# Wait! WHAT?

# MUHAMMAD ALI Was a Chicken?

## DAN GUTMAN

*illustrated by* **ALLISON STEINFELD**

**NORTON YOUNG READERS**

An Imprint of W. W. Norton & Company
Independent Publishers Since 1923

*To kids who like to learn cool stuff.*

For information about permission to reproduce selections from this book, write to
Permissions, W. W. Norton & Company, Inc., 500 Fifth Avenue, New York, NY 10110

For information about special discounts for bulk purchases, please contact
W. W. Norton Special Sales at specialsales@wwnorton.com or 800-233-4830

Manufacturing by Sheridan
Book design by Patrick Collins
Production manager: Anna Oler

Library of Congress Cataloging-in-Publication Data

Names: Gutman, Dan, author. | Steinfeld, Allison, illustrator.
Title: Muhammad Ali was a chicken? / Dan Gutman ; illustrated by Allison Steinfeld.
Description: First edition. | New York : Norton Young Readers, an imprint of
W.W. Norton & Company, [2021] | Series: Wait! what? | Audience: Ages 7–10
Identifiers: LCCN 2020051067 | ISBN 9781324015604 (hardcover) |
ISBN 9781324017066 (paperback) | ISBN 9781324015611 (epub) |
ISBN 9781324016120 (kindle edition)
Subjects: LCSH: Ali, Muhammad, 1942–2016—Juvenile literature. |
Boxers (Sports)—United States--Biography—Juvenile literature.
Classification: LCC GV1132.A4 G88 2021 | DDC 796.83092 [B]—dc23
LC record available at https://lccn.loc.gov/2020051067

W. W. Norton & Company, Inc.
500 Fifth Avenue, New York, N.Y. 10110
www.wwnorton.com

W. W. Norton & Company Ltd.
15 Carlisle Street, London W1D 3BS

2  4  6  8  0  9  7  5  3  1

# CONTENTS

Introduction: That's True, But...      1

Chapter 1: Stuff Your Teacher Wants You to
Know About Muhammad Ali...      7

Chapter 2: Childhood      10

Chapter 3: The Beginning      19

Chapter 4: Selling Tickets      30

Chapter 5: The Greatest      38

Chapter 6: Controversy      45

Chapter 7: Lost Years      53

Chapter 8: Comeback      58

Chapter 9: The Other Side of Ali      71

Chapter 10: Decline      82

Chapter 11: From Hated to Hero      89

Chapter 12: Oh Yeah? (Stuff About Ali
That Didn't Fit Anywhere Else)      98

To Find Out More...      103

Acknowledgments      105

## A WORD FROM PAIGE & TURNER

Muhammad Ali spent his first twenty-two years with the name "Cassius Clay" before changing it. Sometimes we're going to call him Muhammad Ali and sometimes we're going to call him Cassius Clay. It's the same person. We'll try not to be confusing.

Too late!

# That's True, But…

I doubt it. I know a lot about Ali.

But you don't know this.

Please excuse my brother. Turner and I have always been interested in famous people. We thought it would be cool to choose some celebrities and learn all about them. But we didn't want to learn regular, boring stuff about famous people that you can find anywhere. We want to learn about unusual stuff. Odd stuff. Strange stuff. Funny stuff.

Yeah, the stuff you don't see in regular biographies. I'll give you an example. Did you know that in the middle of one bout, Muhammad Ali had a load of ice cubes dropped down his pants?

Wait! What? How do you know that? I didn't come across that in my research.

It's true. He was fighting against Henry Cooper in 1966, and he was losing. He looked dazed and confused. So his cornermen dumped ice cubes down his pants to wake him up. Then Ali went on to win the bout.

That's cool, in more ways than one.

See? I know lots of stuff *you* don't know about Muhammad Ali. Do you want to hear about the guy who licked his sweat?

No! Yuck! That's disgusting!

Okay, I'll save it for later. I guess we should start this book off by saying the obvious—Muhammad Ali was a chicken.

Turner! He was not!

Was too. It says so on the cover of this book. It *must* be true.

Nobody asked *me* what the title should be.

Well, it's too late to change it now. But it doesn't matter, because Muhammad Ali really *was* a chicken.

You're nuts! He was the heavyweight champion of the world. Three times! Nobody *ever* did that before.

He was a chicken, I say.

You're crazy. Do you even know what it *means* to be the heavyweight champion? It means you're fearless. Nobody can beat you.

Buck buck buck!

Is that your chicken imitation? It's terrible. Look, Muhammad Ali was one of the most important sports figures in history. He was named Sportsman of the Century by *Sports Illustrated*. He was awarded the Presidential Medal of Freedom. His boxing career spanned seven presidents. He was probably the most recognizable person on the planet.

So what? I still say he was a chicken.

You can't just make a crazy statement like that, Turner. You have to back it up with *facts*. That's what this book is all about. Do you even know what nonfiction means?

4

Sure I do. You want the truth? Okay, here's the truth. Muhammad Ali didn't like to fly. After one really bumpy flight, he decided he wouldn't get on a plane again. But the 1960 Olympics were coming up and he wanted to win the gold medal. He told his coach he would only go to the Olympics in Rome if he could take a boat there. Well, the coach said no way. They had a long talk. The coach told Ali that if he wanted to have a career in boxing, he would have to get over his fear of flying. So Ali did the logical thing.

He got on the plane?

Yeah. But first he bought a parachute so he could wear it during the flight to Rome!

You're kidding me! That is hilarious.

It also proves my point. Muhammad Ali was a chicken. Oooh, I just took my sister to school!

You did not! *Lots* of people are afraid of flying. That doesn't make them chickens.

Buck buck buck!

We'll just have to agree to disagree on this one.

Fine. But I just proved that I know facts you don't. That reminds me, did you know it's impossible to hum while you're holding your nose?

CHAPTER 1

# Stuff Your Teacher Wants You to Know About Muhammad Ali…

**January 17, 1942** Born in Louisville, Kentucky.

**October 1954** Begins boxing lessons.

**September 1960** Wins gold medal as a light heavyweight at the 1960 Olympics in Rome.

**October 1960** Wins first professional bout.

**1964** Wins world heavyweight title, converts to Islam, changes name from Cassius Clay to Muhammad Ali.

**1967** Refuses to be inducted into the United States Army. Is convicted of draft evasion, stripped of his title, and banned from boxing.

**1970** Wins return match against Jerry Quarry.

**1971** The Supreme Court reverses his conviction. He loses for the first time as a professional, to Joe Frazier.

**1974** Wins heavyweight title for the second time, beating George Foreman in Zaire.

**1975** Wins "Thrilla in Manila" against Joe Frazier in Quezon City, Philippines.

**1978** Loses heavyweight crown for the second time, to Leon Spinks. Wins heavyweight crown for the *third* time, beating Spinks seven months later.

**1981** Retires from boxing.

**1984** Diagnosed with Parkinson's syndrome.

**1996** Lights torch at Summer Olympics in Atlanta.

**June 3, 2016** Dies in Scottsdale, Arizona.

Still awake? Great! Okay, let's get to the *good* stuff, the stuff your *teacher* doesn't even know about Muhammad Ali…

# CHAPTER 2
# Childhood

When Muhammad Ali was born at 6:35 p.m. on January 17, 1942, in Louisville City Hospital, the doctor used a tool called a "forceps." It made a small mark on Ali's right cheek that stayed there for the rest of his life.

Ali's birth name was Cassius Marcellus Clay. But on the birth certificate, it was misspelled as "Cassuis."

His father's name was *also* Cassius Marcellus Clay. What an amazing coincidence!

# 10 PEOPLE
## Born on
## Ali's Birthday

**VIDAL SASSOON**
British-American Hair Stylist
1928

**EARTHA KITT**
Singer, Dancer
& Actress
1927

**MACK SENNETT**
Movie Pioneer
1880

**BETTY WHITE**
Actress & Comedian
1922

**JIM CARREY**
Comedian & Actor
1962

**BENJAMIN FRANKLIN**
Founding Father
1706

**MICHELLE OBAMA**
First Lady
1964

**JAMES EARL JONES**
Actor
1931

**ARNOLD ROTHSTEIN**
Gambler & Mobster
1882

**AL CAPONE**
Gangster
1899

11

They planned it that way, you dope!

I'm just messing with you. In the hospital, Ali cried so much that it made all the other babies near him start crying too.

Ali's great-grandfather was an enslaved person. He belonged to the family of senator Henry Clay of Kentucky.

Ali's father made his living painting signs. His mother, Odessa Grady Clay, was a house cleaner. Her nickname was Bird. The two parents argued over what to name the baby. His father liked "Rudolph," in honor of movie star Rudolph Valentino. But his mother insisted on "Cassius."

Less than two years later, they had another baby boy. Guess what they named him.

Rudolph?

Bingo.

They named their son Bingo?

No! They named him Rudolph.

That's what I said!

# 7 THINGS
## That happened on
## Ali's Birthday

**1773** Captain James Cook becomes the first person to cross the Antarctic Circle.

**1912** Captain Robert Scott's expedition arrives at the South Pole.

**1920** Prohibition begins.

**1929** The cartoon character Popeye first appears.

**1946** The United Nations Security Council holds its first session.

**1949** The first Volkswagen Beetle arrives in the United States from Germany.

**1950** Eleven thieves steal almost $3 million from a Brink's armored car in Boston.

Ali's family wasn't wealthy. Most of his clothes came from Goodwill. His parents put cardboard linings inside his shoes so they would last longer.

The shoes or the parents?

The shoes! Ali went to Virginia Avenue Elementary School in Louisville. One of his report cards said he was interested in art.

Ali loved to eat. His breakfast was a quart of milk mixed with two raw eggs.

GULP! GULP!

Yuck!

He would eat his lunch on the way to school, and then talk other kids into sharing their food with him at lunchtime. When he was in high school, he needed two trays to carry his lunch. He never drank soda because he knew it was bad for him. But he would drink six bottles of milk during one meal.

Double yuck!

Ali would play touch football with kids at school, but he didn't like tackle football. He wasn't interested in team sports.

But he was good at marbles.

What's that?

It's a game kids used to play. Google it. As a young man, Ali would earn money by babysitting. He also worked as a part-time janitor.

Did you know that when he was a kid, Ali had a pet chicken and a black dog named Rusty?

Everybody knows that. Did you know that he got measles and chicken pox at the same time?

Everybody knows that. But here's some stuff hardly *anybody* knows…

# 9 LITTLE KNOWN
## Things About
## Ali's Childhood

+ His first bout was against his mother. When he was two years old, he accidentally socked her in the mouth and knocked out one of her teeth.

+ Instead of taking the bus to school, he would run to school, racing against the school bus.

+ Ali and his brother shared a bedroom, and they had a secret language where they would communicate by clucking their tongues.

- Ali would ask his brother to throw rocks at him, and then dodge the flying rocks.

- Other kids made fun of Ali and his brother by saying they had big heads.

- For fun, Ali and friends would hide in an alley and roll old tires into the street in front of passing cars.

- He could imitate the sound of a police siren and make cars pull over to the side of the road.

- One day in high school, he showed up wearing lipstick and carrying a purse to pretend he was a girl.

- He had a recurring dream that he was running down the street when a truck suddenly came straight at him. In the dream, he would wave his arms, fly over the truck, and keep flying.

HONK!

HONK!

When he was twelve, Ali tried boxing for the first time. It all began...Well, this seems like a good place to start a new chapter in this book, and a new chapter in Ali's life.

"Don't count the days; MAKE THE DAYS COUNT."

# CHAPTER 3

# The Beginning

This is a great story. They should make it into a movie.

Yeah. It all started on Christmas morning in 1953, when eleven-year-old Cassius Clay woke up and found a brand-new bicycle next to the Christmas tree. It was a beautiful thing—a red and white Schwinn Cruiser Deluxe with a headlight that was shaped like a rocket. His parents didn't have a lot of money, so this was a really special gift.

Having a bike meant independence! You could get around without having to rely on your mom or dad to drive you. Cassius loved his new bike.

A few months later, he and one of his friends were riding their bikes around Louisville. It started raining. The boys left their bikes outside and went in the Columbia Auditorium, where a big expo was going on. Vendors were giving away candy, so the boys grabbed some. When they came back outside, the rain had stopped, but the Schwinn was gone. Somebody had stolen it.

I would have freaked out!

That's exactly what Cassius did. He started crying. He was probably most upset that his parents were going to punish him for coming home without his bike.

Somebody said he should report it to the police, so the boys went back inside. There was a police station in there. The officer they spoke to was named Joe Martin. And this was a moment that would change the life of Cassius Clay.

"Somebody stole my bike," he said. "When I find out who did it, I'm going to beat him up good."

Officer Martin looked at the eighty-nine-pound kid.

"Do you know how to fight?" he asked. "You better learn how to fight before you start challenging people."

As it turned out, in his spare time, Joe Martin taught boxing to boys in Louisville. He invited Cassius to come to his gym so he could show him the ropes.

I get it! Show him the ropes!

Cassius went to the gym, and he liked what he saw—guys working out, hitting punching bags, skipping rope. So he went back a second time.

Wow!

That's when he stepped into a boxing ring for the first time. It didn't go well. The other kid was older and more

21

experienced. Cassius got beaten up badly. He was dizzy. His mouth hurt, and his nose was bleeding.

But it didn't put him off. He became obsessed with boxing. After that, he would doodle pictures of boxing rings and boxing gloves in his notebooks at school. He would pretend that announcements over the loudspeaker were saying, "Cassius Clay, heavyweight champion of the world." He would give out autographs to kids—*Cassius Clay, World Heavyweight Champ.*

Of course, dreams won't make you the champion of *anything*. You've got to work. Cassius started training at Joe Martin's gym six days a week. He worked *really* hard. He never drank, smoked, or took drugs. All he cared about was boxing. Joe Martin knew Cassius was special.

Cassius had his first bout in November 1954 against a boy named Ronnie O'Keefe. They fought three rounds. Cassius won, and he began competing in local boxing tournaments, coached by Joe Martin. He fought twelve bouts

I hated every minute of training, but I said, 'DON'T QUIT. Suffer now and live the rest of your life as a CHAMPION.'

in 1957. After each one, he would cut stories about himself out of the newspaper and paste them in his scrapbook. He was becoming well-known around Louisville.

But school was not a priority for Cassius Clay. He wasn't good in math, and he was a poor reader. He probably had dyslexia, although hardly anybody knew about dyslexia in those days. Years later, two of his children were dyslexic.

Cassius missed a lot of school because he was traveling to boxing tournaments. Some of his teachers at Central High School didn't think he should graduate. But the principal, Atwood Wilson, saw something in Cassius. He stood up at a faculty meeting and told the teachers that Cassius just might become  famous someday. If he did, their claim to fame would be that they taught him as a teenager. The teachers agreed to let Cassius get his diploma, and he graduated 376th in a class of 391 students.

Cassius fought a hundred and eight bouts as an amateur, winning almost all of them. Meanwhile, he was adding weight, muscle, and strength to his body. By 1960, he had become a heavyweight—the biggest, heaviest category in boxing.

The thing is, Cassius Clay didn't look or fight like other heavyweights. They were usually big and slow. They didn't move fast or gracefully, the way Cassius did. They didn't dance around the ring.

Many boxing experts doubted whether Cassius could be a champion. He kept his hands low instead of using them to protect his face. He ducked away from punches instead of blocking them. They didn't think that he could take a hard punch. But nobody knew for sure. He was so fast, other boxers weren't able to hit him.

But in 1959 and 1960, Cassius won the national Golden Gloves titles, the top amateur tournament in the country. He was eighteen, and he was ready to move up to the next level.

The 1960 Olympics would be in Rome, Italy.

## The Olympics

We won't keep you in suspense. You can guess what happened next. Cassius made it to Rome. He didn't even need his parachute.

In his final match, he went up against Zbigniew Pietrzykowski of Poland, who won the bronze medal at the Olympics four years earlier. Cassius beat him. The gold medal was placed around his neck. He was the best amateur boxer in the world.

When he came home after the Olympics, he wore his gold medal everywhere he went, even to bed at night!

I guess he was probably glad that his bicycle was stolen that day when he was twelve.

By the way, Cassius wasn't instantly cured of his fear of flying. At one point, he bought a bus so he wouldn't have to fly so often. He said the good thing about a bus is that when it breaks down, it doesn't fall out of the sky.

But eventually, he did get over it. In fact, as a prank he would grab the intercom on flights and announce, "Ladies and gentlemen, this is the captain speaking. We're having problems with the engine, and we're gonna crash."

One time, Cassius was on a plane and the flight attendant told him to buckle his seat belt.

"Superman don't need no seat belt," he told her.

"Superman don't need no plane," said the flight attendant.

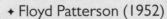

# 5 AMERICAN BOXERS
## Who Won
### Olympic Gold Medals

✦ Floyd Patterson (1952)

✦ Cassius Clay (1960)

✦ Joe Frazier (1964)

✦ George Foreman (1968)

✦ Leon Spinks (1976)

# 8 THINGS
## you Probably didn't know About Boxing

+ Some historians say it's called "boxing" because the ancient Greeks compared a clenched fist with a box.

+ Why is it called a "ring" when it's square? Centuries ago a large circle would be drawn in the dirt when two men had a fistfight. Then the spectators would form a ring around the fighters.

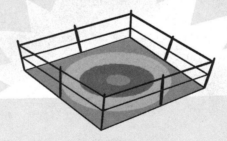

+ Boxing rings aren't all the same size. They range from sixteen to twenty-four square feet, depending on the type of competition.

- The best boxing gloves are made from thin cowhide and filled with horsehair. Less expensive ones are made from synthetic leather or vinyl with foam padding inside.

- Boxing gloves weigh anywhere from four ounces (for kids) all the way up to twenty-four ounces (used just for training).

- Professional boxers usually wear ten-ounce gloves. Amateurs actually wear larger, heavier gloves, because they cause less damage when you get hit by them.

- Boxing became part of the Olympics in 688 BC. Back then, boxers wrapped their hands in leather strips. The Romans added iron, brass, and even a large spike. Ouch!

  You win! You win!

- Jack Broughton, from England, was the inventor of the modern boxing glove. Before that, boxing was only "bare knuckle." Broughton also established the first rules of boxing, in 1743.

# CHAPTER 4

# Selling Tickets

Right after he won the Olympic gold medal, Cassius turned *professional*. That meant he would be paid for boxing. His first pro bout was against thirty-one-year-old Tunney Hunsaker, the police chief of Fayetteville, West Virginia. Cassius won.

If you want to be successful as a professional boxer, you have to put on a show. You have to sell tickets. If nobody comes to see you, you don't make money. Well, Cassius turned out

to be a natural at promoting himself. He loved attention and loved to be loved by people. Even as a teenager, he would go around Louisville knocking on doors and asking people to come see his next bout.

When he was nineteen, Cassius met a pro wrestler named George Raymond Wagner. He went by the name "Gorgeous George." He was an outrageous character who paraded into the arena on a red carpet while his assistants threw rose petals at his feet.

What a *jerk*!

It gets better. Gorgeous George wore a sequined cape and he had dyed blond hair with curlers in it. His fingernails were painted. After he climbed through the ropes, he would spray perfume around the ring. Then he would announce, "If this bum beats me, I'll crawl across the ring and cut off my hair. But that's not gonna happen because I'm the greatest wrestler in the world!"

What a *jerk*!

Yeah, people *hated* him! But it was all a big act to sell tickets. And you know what? Gorgeous George was one of richest and most famous athletes of the 1950s. He made pro wrestling into a popular form of entertainment. And when Gorgeous George met young Cassius Clay, he told him, "A lot of people will pay to see someone shut your mouth." And Cassius said, "This is a *gooood* idea!"

He started doing things no other boxer

had ever done to attract attention to himself.
He would brag about how "pretty" he was. He
invented a dance called the "Ali Shuffle." He
recited poetry.

People come to see me from all around
To see Cassius hit the ground.
Some get mad, some lose their money,
But Cassius is still as sweet as honey.

Cassius became famous for saying, "Float like
a butterfly, sting like a bee. His hands can't hit
what his eyes can't see." But this was his *first*
poem...

To make America the greatest is my goal,
So I beat the Russian, and I beat the Pole,
And for the USA won the Medal of Gold.

People come to see me from all around
To see Cassius hit the ground.
Some get mad, some lose their money,
But Cassius is still as sweet as honey.

I done wrassled with an alligator
I done tusseled with a whale
Only last week I murdered a rock
Injured a stone, hospitalized a brick
I'm so mean I make medicine sick.

# "They All Must Lose
# in the Round I Choose."

Before one bout, against a guy named Willi
Besmanoff, a reporter asked Cassius how the
fight would turn out. He said he would beat
Besmanoff in seven rounds. Sure enough, the
fight ended in the seventh
round. It was the first time
a boxer predicted the round
he would knock out his
opponent, and then did it.

After that, Cassius
started predicting the round he would beat his
opponent, often making it into a poem.

Before he fought Doug Jones, he predicted,
"This boy likes to mix. So he must fall in six."

Before he fought Archie Moore, he predicted,
"When you come to the fight, don't block the
aisle and don't block the door. You will all go
home after round four."

A lot of people thought Cassius was arrogant.
But all that bragging sold tickets. And as Cassius
put it, "It's not bragging if you can back it up."

It helped that Cassius always had a smile on his face. Most boxers were mean, scowling guys. Cassius could get away with saying crazy things because he was handsome and funny.

## Just to Show You What a Promotional Genius He Was...

One day Cassius met a photographer from *Life*, a popular magazine. Cassius asked the photographer to take pictures of him, but the guy said his editors wouldn't put him in the magazine because Cassius wasn't famous enough.

"It's hard to be humble when you're as great as I am."

Cassius asked what kinds of pictures the guy took. He replied that he did a lot of underwater photography. Cassius told him that he actually *trained* underwater, and said that was why he was able to punch so fast.

They got into the hotel pool and Cassius threw punches while the photographer took pictures of him under the water. It became a big photo feature in *Life*.

But the truth was that Cassius made up the whole story about training underwater. He didn't even know how to swim! He just wanted to get his picture in *Life* magazine.

# CHAPTER 5

# The Greatest

 One secret to Cassius Clay's success was his trainer, Angelo Dundee. During World War II, Dundee inspected planes for the Air Force. After the war, he opened up a boxing gym in Miami. He was in Cassius's corner from the time he turned pro until the end of his career.

Okay, guess what Angelo Dundee liked to chew.

🧑 Gum?

🧑 No.

🧑 Tobacco?

🧑 He would chew on a
wad of adhesive tape.

🧑 Yuck!

🧑 Dundee was also afraid of snakes. When Cassius
would go out running, he would sometimes
come back with a piece of rubber or a curvy
stick and chase Dundee around with it.

🧑 Under Dundee's guidance, Cassius was getting
famous for his big mouth and strong fists. He
was beating tougher and tougher opponents.
Finally he earned a shot at the heavyweight
championship of the world.

🧑 The champ back then was Sonny Liston, who
learned to box while he was in jail. He wasn't
fast like Cassius, but he was a really powerful
puncher. Liston had huge shoulders, and he
would put towels under his robe to make them
look even bigger. He was called "The Bear."

39

# 5 MEAN THINGS
## Cassius Clay Said About
## Sonny Liston

- "He's too ugly to be the world champ."

- "The man needs talking lessons. The man needs boxing lessons. And since he's gonna fight me, he needs falling lessons."

- "If Sonny Liston whups me, I'll kiss his feet in the ring, crawl out of the ring on my knees, tell him he's the greatest, and catch the next jet out of the country."

- "After I whup Sonny Liston, I'm gonna whup those little green men from Jupiter and Mars. And looking at them won't scare me none because they can't be no uglier than Sonny Liston."

- "I'm gonna put that ugly bear on the floor, and after the fight I'm gonna build myself a pretty home and use him as a bearskin rug. Liston even smells like a bear. I'm gonna give him to the local zoo after I whup him."

Cassius had never faced an opponent so intimidating. But if he was scared, he didn't show it. Long before the day of the bout, he was bragging that he was going to "whup" Sonny Liston. He even drove his bus from Chicago to Denver just so he could go to Liston's house in the middle of the night and scream at him on the front lawn.

Cassius wrote a poem about the fight...

> I predict that he will go in eight to prove
>     that I'm great.
> And if he wants to go to heaven, I'll get
>     him in seven.
> He'll be in a worser fix if I cut it to six.
> And if he keeps talking jive, I'll cut it
>     to five.
> And if he makes me sore, he'll go like
>     Archie Moore in four.
> And if that don't do, I'll cut it to two.
> And if he run, he'll go in one.
> And if he don't want to fight, he should
>     keep his ugly self home that night.

Well, everybody thought Cassius was going to

41

get stomped by Sonny Liston. forty-three out of forty-six boxing writers picked Liston to win. They said Cassius was a better talker than he was a fighter.

Finally the day of the fight arrived— February 25, 1964. Miami, Florida. It was a huge event. The place was jammed with celebrities. Former heavyweight champ Joe Louis broadcast the play-by-play to movie screens all over America.

Here's a little-known fact: Ali's brother Rudy had his first professional bout that same night. He won.

And here's an even littler-known fact: Before the fight, Cassius asked for two extra tickets. He'd been out on a boat a few days earlier, and it flipped over. Cassius couldn't swim, and some guy pulled him out of the water. Cassius wanted to give him tickets to thank him for saving his life.

Thanks! Do you like boxing?

Nothing very exciting happened during the first three rounds. And then, at the end of the fourth round, Cassius Clay's fight—and with it his career—almost ended. Suddenly he was squinting. He couldn't see. Something was in his eyes. They were burning. He was blinded.

"Cut the gloves off!" he shouted to Angelo Dundee. "We're going home!"

It was probably some ointment on Sonny Liston's body that got in Clay's eyes. He wanted to quit, but Dundee and the other cornermen washed out the eyes and convinced him to keep going.

The fight continued. Liston was getting tired. He was used to knocking guys out in the first round. By round six, Cassius was starting to land punches and dominate the fight.

The bell rang to start the seventh round. Ali got up off the stool in his corner. Liston just sat on his. He spat out his mouth guard. It was over. Cassius Clay, just twenty-two, was the heavyweight champion of the world! He raised his arms and screamed, "I am the greatest!" over and over.

And do you know what was the first thing he did after the fight was over?

He went to the bathroom?

No. He ate a big bowl of vanilla ice cream.

"I am the **GREATEST**! I shook up the world! I'm the greatest thing that ever lived! I'm the king of the world! I'm a bad man! I can't be beat!

I AM KING! KING OF THE WORLD!"

# CHAPTER 6

# Controversy

Cassius shocked the world when he won the heavyweight championship. And the next morning, he shocked the world again, for an entirely different reason.

"I believe in Allah," he announced at a press conference. "I'm not a Christian anymore."

Cassius said he had joined the Nation of Islam and had become a follower of its leader, Elijah Muhammad.

"I don't have to be what you want me to be," he announced. "I'm free to be what I want."

We should make something clear. The "Nation of Islam" and "Islam" aren't the same thing. Islam is an ancient religion practiced by almost two billion people, a quarter of the world's population. The Nation of Islam was a small movement started in 1930 by a man in Detroit.

Elijah Muhammad preached to African Americans that cleanliness, hard work, and independence were what they should strive for.

Why was that controversial?

He also had some ideas that were more extreme. He believed that black people and white people should not live together. He rejected Martin Luther King Jr.'s philosophy of nonviolence. He even told his followers that a "Mother Plane" was hovering in space that was controlled telepathically, and it was going to destroy the earth and all the people on it except for his followers.

Wait. What?

Anyway, Muhammad Ali put his faith in this man and his movement. But we'll talk more about Elijah Muhammad later.

## What's in a name?

"Clay means dirt," Ali announced. "It's the name slave owners gave my people."

When he joined the Nation of Islam, Cassius was given a new name—Muhammad Ali. And from now on in this book, that's what we're going to call him. "Muhammad" means "one worthy of praise." "Ali" was the name of a great general and it also means "lofty."

"Changing my name was one of the most important things that happened to me in my life," Muhammad Ali said later.

Ali's brother Rudy joined the Nation of Islam too. He changed his name to Rahaman Ali.

Lots of people change their names. Ali may be the only person who was famous under two *different* names.

47

# 18 FAMOUS PEOPLE
## Who Changed Their Names

**Marilyn Monroe**—Norma Jean Baker

**Mother Teresa**—Anjezë Gonxhe Bojaxhiu

**Judy Garland**—Frances Ethel Gumm

**John Wayne**—Marion Michael Morrison

**David Bowie**—David Robert Jones

**Bob Dylan**—Robert Allen Zimmerman

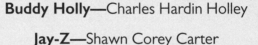

**Billy Holiday**—Eleanora Fagan

**Buddy Holly**—Charles Hardin Holley

**Jay-Z**—Shawn Corey Carter

**Elton John**—Reginald Kenneth Dwight

**Lady Gaga**—Stefani Joanne Angelina Germanotta

**Freddie Mercury**—Farrokh Bulsara

**Ringo Starr**—Richard Starkey

**Stevie Wonder**—Steveland Judkins

**Gerald Ford**—Leslie Lynch King Jr.

**Joseph Stalin**—Iosif Vissarionovich Dzhugashvilli

**Mark Twain**—Samuel Langhorne Clemens

**Lewis Carroll**—Charles Lutwidge Dodgson

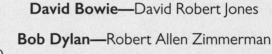
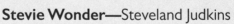
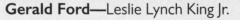

# "I Ain't Got No Quarrel with Them Vietcong."

When you're heavyweight champion, lots of boxers want to take your title away. You have to defend it. Ali took on well-known challengers like Floyd Patterson, and lesser-known boxers like Brian London. He beat them all.

Sonny Liston challenged him, and experts picked Liston to win. But this time Ali knocked him out in the *first* round. It happened so fast that some people went to buy hot dogs, and when they got back to their seats the fight was over!

Ali defended his title nine times in less than two years. Then, suddenly, in 1967, he lost his heavyweight crown...but he didn't lose it to a man.

America was fighting a war in Vietnam. A month before his first fight with Sonny Liston, Ali took a test to see if he was qualified to join the military. He failed the math part of the test, so he wouldn't have to serve.

"I said I was the greatest, not the smartest," Ali joked.

But a lot of people didn't like that decision. Most Americans at the time supported the war. They wanted to know why this young, healthy guy could earn millions of dollars fighting in the boxing ring, but he couldn't fight for his country.

Well, the draft board changed their mind, and it was decided that Ali was eligible to join the military and go to Vietnam.

He announced that he wouldn't go. He said his conscience wouldn't allow him to fight in a war he didn't believe in.

"Why should they ask me to put on a uniform and go ten thousand miles from home and drop bombs and bullets on brown people in Vietnam," he asked, "while so-called Negro people in Louisville are treated like dogs?"

At that time there were places in America where a black man couldn't sit at certain lunch counters, drink from certain water fountains, or stay at certain hotels. African Americans weren't allowed to live in certain neighborhoods, go to certain churches or schools. There wasn't one black U.S. senator or state governor in those days.

If you think about it, a boxing ring was one of the only places where a black man had equal rights. If he hit a white guy in a boxing ring, he wouldn't be arrested, thrown in prison, or worse.

When Ali refused to join the military, it was a big story. People called him a coward and a draft dodger. Many hated him.

"I'll go to jail," he insisted. "We've been in jail for four hundred years."

On April 28, 1967, Ali was ordered to report to the Armed Forces Examining and Entrance Station in Houston, Texas. When his name was called to step forward, he refused. Instead, he made a statement: "I have searched my conscience, and I find I cannot be true to my belief in my religion by accepting such a call."

Ali was arrested and taken away. An hour later, the New York State Athletic Commission took away his boxing license and stripped him of his heavyweight title. He was photographed, fingerprinted, indicted for draft evasion, and convicted.

The punishment was five years in jail.

"If I have to go to jail, I'LL DO IT."

# Lost Years

Muhammad Ali didn't go to jail. He was allowed to remain free while his lawyers appealed the ruling. But he wasn't allowed to box, and he couldn't leave the country. His passport was taken away.

Some people thought it was a publicity stunt. Ali just *said* he was against the war to get attention, like making up silly poems. They said he was…a chicken!

"He who is not **COURAGEOUS** enough to take risks will accomplish nothing in life."

# CHAPTER 7

But look at everything Ali lost by standing up for what he believed. He lost his heavyweight championship, something he had dreamed about since he was a kid. He lost millions of dollars in income. And instead of being loved, he was getting hate mail and death threats every day.

If he was just pretending to be against the war, he did a pretty good job of it.

He had to earn a living, and he got some strange offers. There was a TV sitcom at the time called *Mr. Ed*. It was about a talking horse. For real! They wanted Ali to be on the show. That never happened.

I gotta YouTube that show. There was also talk of Ali playing the boxer Jack Johnson in a play called *The Great White Hope*.

Ali *did* costar with Kris Kristofferson in a four-hour TV mini-series called *Freedom Road*. And he played the title role in a 1969 Broadway musical called *Buck White*. Ali even sang a song called "We Came in Chains."

I'm gonna YouTube that for *sure*.

He was good, but the show closed four days after it opened.

For a while, Ali went on a lecture tour, traveling to colleges all over the country to talk to students about the war and his religious beliefs. But mostly, he waited for the chance to fight again and get his title back.

Here's the interesting thing. In the three years when Ali wasn't allowed to box, people turned against the war in Vietnam. Over fifty-eight thousand American soldiers were killed. More and more people were starting to question why so many teenagers who weren't even old enough to vote were being sent to fight in a foreign country that hadn't attacked America.

So Ali was ahead of his time.

Yes! And in June 1971, four years after he was convicted of draft evasion, the Supreme Court reversed the decision. Ali could return to his career as a professional boxer.

## CHAPTER 8

# Comeback

Most male athletes are at their peak at ages twenty-seven through thirty. That's when their bodies are strongest, and their reflexes fastest. And those were the years when Muhammad Ali was banned from boxing. Imagine how good he would have been if he'd been able to fight when he was in his prime.

58

So there were two Alis. One before the layoff, and one after.

Right. When he returned to boxing, he wasn't quite the same. His legs weren't as quick. He suffered from bursitis, an inflammation of the hands. He had to numb them with medication before each fight.

But he was probably bigger and smarter.

That's true. In his first fight back, he beat Jerry Quarry, a hard puncher from California. Then he beat Oscar Bonavena from Argentina. And after that, he went up against his toughest opponent yet for a shot at the heavyweight title—maybe his toughest opponent *ever*.

## Ali-Frazier

Joe Frazier came from South Carolina. He wasn't fast like Ali and he was barely six feet tall. But he was really strong, he could take a punch, and he was relentless. He was constantly moving forward, and he would wear his opponents down. He was called "Smokin' Joe." Four years after Ali won the Olympic gold medal, Frazier won it.

Ali was undefeated and Frazier was undefeated. For the first time ever, two undefeated heavyweights were fighting for the world championship.

March 8, 1971. Madison Square Garden in New York. The bout was broadcast live to thirty-five countries. It was billed as the "Fight of the Century."

Before the bout, Ali taunted Frazier, calling him ugly and stupid. He filmed himself with one of his training partners wearing a gorilla mask. Frazier knew Ali was just doing these things to sell tickets, but he was still hurt by them.

"How would you like it," Frazier asked, "if your kids came home from school crying, because everyone was calling their daddy a gorilla?"

The Garden was filled with big-name celebrities like Diana Ross, Barbra Streisand, Sammy Davis Jr., Woody Allen, and Miles Davis. Even Colonel Sanders, the founder of KFC, was there!

Bet you don't know who was assigned to take pictures of the bout for *Life* magazine.

I give up.

Frank Sinatra!

The singer? Who knew he could take pictures?

It was a close and brutal fight. At one point

Say Cheese!

in the tenth round, the referee was separating the two fighters when the fingernail of his pinkie caught Frazier in the eye.

"I got two men beating up on me!" Frazier complained.

The fight went the full fifteen rounds. In the last round, Frazier knocked down Ali and was the winner. It was Ali's first loss as a professional boxer.

Bet you didn't know this. Joe Frazier's son *and* his daughter also became boxers. His daughter Jacqui had a 13–1 record. And do you know who was the only fighter who beat her?

I give up.

Muhammad Ali's daughter Laila! She was a boxer too!

Ali didn't quit after he lost to Frazier. He kept fighting and winning, and he kept coming up with ways to promote his bouts. They weren't always good ideas. Before his fight with Buster Mathis in 1971, Ali met with his advisers, trying to come up with a way to get the public excited. It wasn't easy, because the two men seemed to genuinely like each other, and couldn't pretend to be angry.

"I've got it!" Ali shouted. "You can have me kidnapped!"

Ali's idea was to fake his own kidnapping and hide in a cabin in the woods for a few days. Then, just before the fight, he would show up. But he didn't do it. His advisers said people wouldn't buy tickets if they thought he had been kidnapped.

Before his bout with George Foreman in Zaire, a country in Africa, Ali went around shouting, "George Foreman is a Belgian!"

Why?

Because Zaire was once a colony of Belgium, and the people there didn't like Belgians.

# Nicknames

Ali liked giving his opponents nicknames to taunt them. Here are a few...

**George Foreman**—"The Mummy"

**Ernie Terrell**—"The Octopus"

**George Chuvalo**—"The Washerwoman" (Chuvalo actually showed up at the press conference dressed like one.)

**Larry Holmes**—"The Peanut" (Because his head was shaped like one. Ali said, "I'm going to shell him.")

**Antonio Inoki**—"The Pelican"

**Floyd Patterson**—"The Rabbit" (Ali went to Patterson's training camp with lettuce and carrots. "When he's lying there," Ali said, "I'm going to stick a carrot in his mouth.")

Speaking of nicknames, Ali himself was sometimes nicknamed "Mighty Mouth," "The Louisville Lip," or "Cassius the Gaseous." For a short time he grew a mustache and called himself "Dark Gable."

When he was a baby, Ali's first word was, "Gee." So his parents nicknamed him "GG." When he was a grown man, his mother called him "tinky baby" and "woody baby."

## Ali's Squad

Every pro boxer needs a team of people to do stuff for him—train him, drive him around, manage his business. With every fight, Ali seemed to have more people around: Bodyguards. Masseurs. A personal chef. Some were old friends or people Ali met who needed a job. He couldn't say no to anybody. At one point, he hired a professional drummer whose job was to bang a drum whenever Ali landed a punch. He even had a personal magician.

Wait. What?

Ali *loved* magic. One day he was at a mall in

Pennsylvania when he saw a guy doing magic tricks. His name was Terry La Sorda, and he happened to be a cousin of Tommy Lasorda, the manager of the Los Angeles Dodgers. Ali hired La Sorda to teach him tricks. Ali loved to entertain people with card tricks, making handkerchiefs disappear, and levitating his body. But unlike other magicians, he would show how he did his tricks, because he believed that deceiving people was wrong.

Pick a card!

But the weirdest job in Ali's entourage…are you ready for this?

Should I be?

Yeah, you'd better sit down.

Okay, I'm sitting down. Wait. Oh no, I think

I know what you're going to say. You've been waiting the whole book for this moment.

🙂 That's right! Ali had an official…sweat taster!

😮 No, don't say it!

🙂 Yes, this guy's job was to taste Ali's sweat after a workout to see how salty it was.

Ugh, gross! I hope that guy got paid really well.

After losing that first fight to Joe Frazier, Ali was determined to regain the heavyweight championship. He beat Jimmy Ellis, his old sparring partner. He beat Jerry Quarry and Floyd Patterson again. One by one they fell: Buster Mathis, Jürgen Blin, Mac Foster, George Chuvalo, Al Lewis, Bob Foster, Joe Bugner, and Rudie Lubbers. Ali lost to Ken Norton, but beat him in a rematch.

Ali even beat Joe Frazier in a rematch. But Frazier was no longer the champ at that point, because he had been beaten by George Foreman.

Finally, on October 30, 1974, Ali beat Foreman in a fight known as the "Rumble in the Jungle" because it was held in Zaire, and became heavyweight champion for a *second* time. This would have been the perfect moment to retire and go down in history as one of the greatest boxers ever.

And…

He didn't.

# 2 GREAT FACTS
## about George Forman

+ He had five sons, and named all of them George.

+ In 1994, a kitchen appliance called the "George Foreman Lean Mean Fat-Reducing Grilling Machine" was introduced. Foreman said, "It's so good I put my name on it." A hundred million of the grills were sold. Foreman earned over two hundred million dollars! That's way more than he earned boxing.

"Only a man who knows what it is like to be defeated can reach down to the bottom of his soul and come up with the extra ounce of power it takes to win when the match is even."

# CHAPTER 9

# The Other Side of Ali

Most boxers are famous just for boxing. But with his good looks, quick wit, and big mouth, Ali might have become a celebrity even if he never had a fight. He had already done TV and appeared on Broadway. So of course it was time for...

# Movies

Ali loved movies (especially westerns and horror films) and the camera loved him. There are lots of documentaries about him (check YouTube). Ali played himself in *The Greatest* (1977), which also starred James Earl Jones (the voice of Darth Vader). Will Smith played Ali in the 2001 movie *Ali*.

There were other movie offers that never worked out. In 1972, Ali was approached about starring in *Heaven Can Wait*, a movie about a boxer who's brought back to life after he dies. Ali decided not to do the film because Muslims don't believe in life after death. It became a hit with Warren Beatty as the star.

In 1975, Ali fought a liquor salesman from Bayonne, New Jersey, named Chuck Wepner. It should have been an easy knockout, but Wepner lasted into the fifteenth round.

An unknown actor named Sylvester Stallone was watching that bout on TV. He spent the next twenty hours writing a script about a second-rate boxer who survives fifteen rounds against the heavyweight champion of the world. The movie was called *Rocky*. It made Stallone a star and won the Oscar for Best Picture. There have been seven sequels!

And Chuck Wepner? He appeared with Ali in a short film for kids, about dental hygiene. Ali knocked out "Mr. Tooth Decay"—Wepner.

## Music

As a teenager, Ali idolized Elvis Presley. The two met in 1973, and Elvis gave Ali a robe with "People's Champion" spelled out in rhinestones on the back. Ali wore it as he came into the ring for two fights. Then Ken Norton broke Ali's jaw, and Ali stopped wearing the robe.

In 1963, just before he beat Sonny Liston, Ali recorded an album titled *I Am the Greatest*. (You can listen to it on Spotify.) He recites a bunch of corny jokes, skits, and poems like...

*The punch raises Liston*
*Clear out of the ring.*
*Liston is still rising*
*And the ref wears a frown,*
*For he can't start counting,*
*Till Sonny comes down.*
*Now Liston disappears from view.*
*The crowd is getting frantic,*
*But our radar stations have picked him up.*
*He's somewhere over the Atlantic.*
*Who would have thought*
*When they came to the fight*
*That they'd witness the launching*
*Of a human satellite?*
*Yes, the crowd did not dream*
*When they put down their money*
　　　　　　　*That they would see*
　　　　　　　*A total eclipse*
　　　　　　　　*of the Sonny!*

You should listen to that album just to hear Ali sing the classic song "Stand By Me."

By the way, Ali wasn't the only boxer who thought he could sing. Joe Frazier led a soul-funk group called Joe Frazier and the Knockouts. And Ernie Terrell, who fought Ali in 1967, had a group called Ernie Terrell and the Heavyweights.

## 4 SONGS
### Inspired by Ali

+ "The Greatest Love of All" was a hit for George Benson and Whitney Houston. It was written for the 1977 movie about Ali called *The Greatest*.

+ "Cassius Clay" (1973) by Jamaican reggae singer Dennis Alcapone

+ "Black Superman" (1975) by British singer Johnny Wakelin

+ "The Louisville Lip" (1971) by singer-songwriter Eddie Curtis

You can watch videos of all these on YouTube.

# Money

Ali earned fifty to a hundred *million* dollars in his career. For just one fight against Joe Frazier, Ali was paid nine million. That's a lot of cash for one night's work!

Just to compare, in 1967 the average NFL player earned twenty-five thousand dollars a year. NBA players made even less, about twenty thousand.

Ali didn't like checks. He liked cash. One time, he went to the bank to take out twenty-seven thousand one-dollar bills. The bank gave him a big sack of money. He took it back to his hotel room, dumped all the bills on the bed, and counted them. The total was a thousand dollars short. So Ali took the money back to the bank to get the full amount.

Ali earned a lot of money, but he also spent a lot. He had to pay lawyers and taxes, employees and hangers-on. He bought lots of cars—the first thing he did after turning pro was buy a pink Cadillac. There was alimony for his ex-wives and child support for his kids. He made some bad business deals. He gave money

to people who asked for help. At one point, he had a hundred and nine dollars in his bank account.

Ali could have retired at the top. But it's hard to quit when you're the best in the world at what you do and people are offering you millions to keep doing it. And people offered him money to do some strange things...

## Strange Fights!

In 1976 somebody had the idea to stage a fight between Ali and Japanese wrestler Antonio Inoki. It was billed as the "Martial Arts Championship of the World." Inoki got down on the mat and kicked Ali's legs

for fifteen rounds. Ali hopped around avoiding Inoki. He only threw six punches. It was boring. Spectators threw garbage into the ring. The fight ended as a draw. When it was over, Ali had ruptured blood vessels in his legs and had to go to the hospital.

In 1969 Ali was in a simulated "computer fight" against ex-champion Rocky Marciano, who had been retired for thirteen years. Marciano lost forty pounds and wore a toupee to look younger. The boxers were filmed sparring and then the film was edited according to a computer prediction of who would have won. In the version shown in theaters in the U.S., Marciano won—but he never found out. He died in a plane crash three weeks after filming was over.

Wilt Chamberlain was one of the greatest basketball players of his time, but he also dreamed of fighting for the heavyweight championship of the world. So Ali agreed to give him a shot. Chamberlain had never boxed before.

He was called "Wilt the Stilt" because he was

seven-foot-two. When he walked into the press
conference to announce the fight, Ali shouted,
"Timber!" (which lumberjacks shout as a tree is
about to fall down). Wilt changed his mind and
backed out of the fight.

Ali was visiting Uganda in the 1970s when
President Idi Amin offered half a million dollars
to fight him. Amin was one of the cruelest
rulers in history and was called the "Butcher
of Uganda." It was said that he pointed a gun
at Ali to convince him to fight. Ali left Uganda
instead.

# Roach traps?

People were constantly approaching Ali to endorse products. He appeared in ads for clothing, toys, shoe polish, cologne, bedsheets, and exercise equipment. There was the Muhammad Ali Peanut Butter Crisp Crunch candy bar. There were comic books (*Superman vs. Muhammad Ali: The Fight to Save Earth from Star-Warriors*) and an animated TV series (*The Adventures of Muhammad Ali*) where he wrestled alligators and fought space aliens. There was soda ("Mr. Champs") and hamburger joints (Champburger). He endorsed Bulova watches, Ore-Ida hash brown potatoes, and d-CON roach traps.

Toward the end of his life, Ali's wife Lonnie took charge of his business interests and started a company called G.O.A.T. (Greatest of All Time) to manage his finances. The company was sold in 2006 for fifty million dollars.

"I really want to quit. But if someone offers you ten million, it ain't easy."

# CHAPTER 10

# Decline

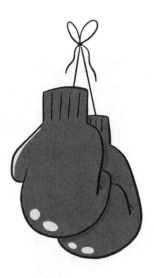

People get injured in all sports. But in boxing the *purpose* of the sport is to hurt the other guy. Knock him down. Knock him *out*. If a player gets hurt in a team sport like football or baseball, they bring in a sub. Not in boxing. It's just you. And you're not wearing a helmet, shoulder pads, or other protection.

During his career, it was estimated that Ali took about two hundred thousand punches to his body and head. People started saying Ali should retire, but he didn't. Boxing was all he knew, and the money was good. But the human brain is delicate.

## Rope-a-Dope

As he got older, Ali couldn't dance around and use speed to win fights. So he tried a different strategy. He would lean against the ropes, cover his head with his hands, and just let his opponent hit him over and over again. The other boxer would eventually get tired, and then Ali would fight back and win. He called it "rope-a-dope."

Sometimes it worked. But it was boring to watch. Worse than that, Ali's head and body took a tremendous amount of punishment while he was roping dopes.

Fun fact: Companies started selling Muhammad Ali Rope-a-Dope-Soap-on-a-Rope!

Ali not only took a pounding in the ring, he also let his training partners hit him in the head. In fact, he *insisted* on it. He thought it helped him prepare for his fights.

"You gotta condition your body and brain to take those shots," he said.

After a fight against Ernie Shavers in 1977, a lab report showed his kidneys were failing. Madison Square Garden stopped offering him bouts. Ali's doctor, Ferdie Pacheco, quit. But Ali wouldn't quit. He was still winning fights in 1976 and 1977, even though he was in his mid-thirties.

Then, in 1978, he defended his title against twenty-five-year-old Leon Spinks in Las Vegas. Spinks only had seven pro fights. It should have been an easy win for Ali. But Spinks shocked everybody by beating Ali and taking his title.

After it was over, Spinks imitated Ali with a little poetry: "Ali's the greatest; I'm just the latest."

Ali announced he was retiring, but he didn't. He beat Spinks in a rematch. Then was beaten badly by Larry Holmes in 1980.

## Ali's Last fight:
## The Drama in Bahama

It was December 11, 1981. Ali's fortieth birthday was a month away. He was slow and heavy, and he had started dyeing his gray hair. Ali lost the fight with Trevor Berbick, from Jamaica.

"I'm finished," Ali said after it was over. "You can't beat Father Time. I'll never fight again."

This time, he meant it.

Ali had fifty-six pro fights. He lost five of them...

+ Joe Frazier (1971)

+ Ken Norton (1973)

+ Leon Spinks (1978)

+ Larry Holmes (1980)

+ Trevor Berbick (1981)

# Parkinson's

Ali's doctor, Ferdie Pacheco, said he noticed brain damage in Ali after his fight against Joe Frazier in 1971. By 1978, friends noticed that Ali was slurring his words when he spoke. It was getting worse every year. He started walking slowly. He would fall asleep in the middle of conversations, or forget who he was talking to on the phone. His voice, which was once so loud, became faint. His hands, which were once so powerful, trembled.

Finally, in 1984, Ali was diagnosed with Parkinson's syndrome. He was forty-two.

Parkinson's is a disorder of the central nervous system caused by nerve cell damage in the brain. There are treatments to help patients, but there's no cure.

That didn't stop Ali from looking. He saw a Mexican surgeon who offered a treatment that involved removing cells from the adrenal gland and transplanting them into the brain. A Yugoslavian doctor told Ali his problem was that he had pesticides in his blood. He offered a blood-cleansing treatment that was supposed to eliminate the toxins. One of Ali's doctors diagnosed a thyroid problem and gave Ali drugs to correct it.

"I don't want anyone to feel sorry for me, because I had a good life before, and I'm having a good life now."

It's very possible that Ali's Parkinson's was a result of getting hit in the head for thirty years. But many people who never boxed get Parkinson's.

I guess we'll never know why Ali got it.

# CHAPTER 11

# From Hated to Hero

Some famous people avoid their fans. They think shaking hands and signing autographs are a nuisance. In 1960, Ali got the brush-off when he met one of his heroes, boxer Sugar Ray Robinson.

"If I ever get great and famous and people want my autograph enough to wait all day to see me," Ali said, "I'm sure goin' to treat 'em different."

So he did. Besides giving countless autographs and hugs, he answered hundreds of letters. He would go to hospitals to cheer up sick kids when no TV cameras were around. He would drive through poor neighborhoods and buy dinner for homeless people.

Ali would leave his hotel with five hundred dollars in his wallet and come back with nothing, because he gave all the money away. Strangers would come from all over the world, show up at his door, and Ali would invite them inside.

Here are more examples of Ali's generosity…

✦ **In 1966,** Teddy Waltham was paid twenty-four hundred dollars in cash to referee one of Ali's fights. On his way home, somebody picked Waltham's pocket and stole the money. When Ali found out, he gave Waltham twenty-four hundred.

+ **In 1975,** Ali saw on TV that a Jewish community center for senior citizens and Holocaust survivors was going to close because it ran out of money. Ali wrote them a check for a hundred thousand dollars.

+ **In 1977,** Ali saw a homeless man in New York and gave him a hundred-dollar bill. Ali realized the man might have trouble spending such a big bill, so he offered him five twenties instead. The man didn't want to let go of the hundred. He said he'd never seen one before. So Ali let him keep the hundred *and* the twenties.

+ **In 1981,** Ali was in Los Angeles when he heard a man was threatening to jump out the window of a tall building. Ali rushed over and talked the guy down off the ledge. The next day, Ali visited him in the hospital and promised to help him buy clothes and find a job.

Ali loved people, and it showed. That's one reason why he went from being one of the most controversial people in America to one of the most loved.

The other reason is that over the years, the United States changed. Many people came to believe the Vietnam War was a mistake and Ali was right to refuse to join the military.

Also, Elijah Muhammad died (in 1975) and the Nation of Islam became less radical. They got rid of dress codes and a ban against dancing. People of any race were allowed to join. Ali said, "I've changed what I believe."

At the end of his life, he regretted some of the things he had said and done when he was younger. He told the *New York Times*: "I said a lot of things in the heat of the moment that I shouldn't have said. I apologize for that. I'm sorry. It was all meant to promote the fight."

When the nation was attacked on 9/11,

Ali announced, "I am an American. Whoever performed, or is behind, the terrorist attacks in the United States of America does not represent Islam."

By that time, he had become an American hero. He served as the United Nations Messenger of Peace. He was sent on a mission to Iraq with the hope that he could help prevent a war there.

President Ford invited him to the White House. President Carter considered having Ali negotiate the release of hostages in Iran. President George W. Bush presented him with the Presidential Medal of Freedom.

After being born a grandson of enslaved people, Ali went to the inauguration of the first African American president, Barack Obama.

Toward the end of Ali's life, his boyhood home in Louisville had become a museum, and a bigger museum was built downtown to honor him. The main street was renamed Muhammad Ali Boulevard. The airport is named after him. One of the streets outside New York's Madison Square Garden is called Muhammad Ali Way.

And in 1999, Ali received the ultimate honor—his picture was on the Wheaties box.

## Back to the Olympics

Frank Sadlo was an old friend of Ali's family. In 1994, he was working as a waiter at an Applebee's restaurant in Louisville. Sadlo thought the upcoming 1996 Olympics in Atlanta would be the perfect time to celebrate Ali's life. He wrote dozens of letters and made

94

hundreds of phone calls trying to get Olympic officials interested in the idea.

When the opening ceremony took place on June 19, the big mystery was: Who would light the Olympic torch?

Lots of people thought it would be Hank Aaron of the Atlanta Braves, who had hit seven hundred and fifty-five home runs in his baseball career.

The crowd let out a roar when the boxer Evander Holyfield carried a torch into the stadium. He handed it to Janet Evans, who won four Olympic gold medals for swimming. She jogged to the base of the big Olympic torch.

And then, out from the shadows stepped Muhammad Ali. People went *crazy*.

Ali held the torch with his right hand. His left hand was shaking from Parkinson's. Janet Evans brought her flaming torch to light Ali's torch. Ali bent down slowly to light a wick. He was struggling. It looked like he might set his clothes on fire.

But suddenly the wick caught fire and the flame shot up to the top of the stadium to ignite the torch. It was one of the most dramatic moments in Olympic history.

When Ali was young, he looked like a superhero who could do anything and feel no pain. At the end of his life, suffering from a crippling disease, he seemed more human, with real human problems. People related to him, and loved him even more.

Muhammad Ali died at 9:10 p.m. on June third, 2016, in Scottsdale, Arizona. He was seventy-four. He's buried in Cave Hill Cemetery in Louisville.

Boxing made him famous, and probably also shortened his life. We'll never know what would have happened if Ali hadn't spent his life fighting. He might still be with us today.

 But if he hadn't spent his life fighting, we wouldn't be talking, writing, or reading about him either.

"Live everyday as if it were your last because someday you're going to be right."

# CHAPTER 12

# Oh Yeah? (Stuff About Ali That Didn't Fit Anywhere Else)

We haven't talked much about Ali's personal life.

Who cares about that?

Some kids care! Actually, Ali was very shy. At the 1959 Golden Gloves tournament, he kept bugging the other boxers to go out dancing and meet girls. But when they finally agreed, Ali didn't dance or say a word to any girls. He was too embarrassed.

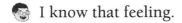 I know that feeling.

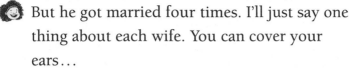 But he got married four times. I'll just say one thing about each wife. You can cover your ears...

1. **Sonji Roi: 1964.** The first words he said to her were, "Girl, will you marry me?" They got married forty-one days later.

2. **Belinda Boyd: 1967.** They had four children. She had a small part in the Jane Fonda movie *The China Syndrome*.

3. **Veronica Porché: 1977.** She was hired to promote the Ali-Foreman fight in Zaire. They had two daughters.

4. **Lonnie Williams: 1986.** They met way back in 1963, when their families lived across the street from each other in Louisville. Ali was twenty-one years old then, and Lonnie was just six. But they kept in touch, and almost a quarter

century later, they got married. He was ill by that time, and Lonnie took care of him for the rest of his life.

So after traveling the world, Ali ended up marrying the girl next door. Isn't that romantic?

No. But did you know that in the 1980s, Ali and Lonnie moved to a farm in Michigan that was once owned by the gangster Al Capone?

Everybody knows that. Did you know the last boxer to get knocked down by Ali was Richard Dunn, in 1976?

Of course! You think you know everything. But I'll tell you something you don't know. Ali was fast with his hands, but not so fast on his feet. The Olympic sprinter Wilma Rudolph was visiting Louisville in 1960 and Ali challenged her to a race. She beat him easily. And in 1977, Ali raced against Marvin Gaye, Tony Orlando,

> **"It isn't the mountains ahead to climb that wear you out; it's the pebble in your shoe."**

and other celebrities in the Muhammad Ali Invitational Track Meet. Ali finished second to last.

Oh yeah? Ali once told a reporter that he never read a book in his life. And that included his autobiography, *The Greatest: My Own Story.*

Oh yeah? Ali liked to judge things according to their *weight*. When people came to visit his house, he would tell them to pick up knickknacks to show how heavy they were.

# TO FIND OUT MORE...

 Did we get you interested in the life of Muhammad Ali? Yay! You can watch hundreds of videos of Ali boxing (and talking) on YouTube. And there are many other books for kids about him. Ask if your librarian has these...

✦ *I Shook Up the World: The Incredible Life of Muhammad Ali* (2004) by Maryum "Maymay" Ali

✦ *Champion: The Story of Muhammad Ali* by Jim Haskins (2018)

✦ *Muhammad Ali* by Josh Gregory (2017)

✦ *I Am Muhammad Ali* by Felicia S. Hudson (2017)

✦ *Ali: An America Champion* by Barry Denenberg (2014)

- *Twelve Rounds to Glory: The Story of Muhammad Ali* by Charles R. Smith Jr. (2010)

- *Muhammad Ali: King of the Ring* by Stephen Timblin (2010)

- *Muhammad Ali: The Greatest* by Susan Brophy Down (2013)

- *Muhammad Ali: The Life of a Boxing Hero* by Rob Shone (2006)

- *Muhammad Ali: Genius* by Nick Healy (2005)

- *The Greatest: Muhammad Ali* by Walter Dean Myers (2001)

- *Muhammad Ali: The King of the Ring* by Lewis Helfand (2012)

# ACKNOWLEDGMENTS

Thanks to Simon Boughton, Allison Steinfeld, Liza Voges, and Nina Wallace. The facts in this book came from many books, videos, and other sources. Especially helpful were *Muhammad Ali* by Thomas Hauser, and *Ali* by Jonathan Eig.

# ABOUT THE AUTHOR

Dan Gutman has written many books for young readers, such as: My Weird School, The Genius Files, Flashback Four, *The Kid Who Ran for President*, *The Homework Machine*, *The Million Dollar Shot*, and the Baseball Card Adventure series. Dan and his wife Nina live New York City. You can find out more about Dan and his books by visiting his website (www.dangutman.com) or following him on Facebook, Twitter, or Instagram.

TITLES IN THE

Wait! WHAT?

SERIES

*Albert Einstein Was a Dope?*

*Muhammad Ali Was a Chicken?*

*Amelia Earhart Is on the Moon?*